the TECHNOLOGY beHIND

THE INTERNET

Nicolas Brasch

- ➲ What Is the Difference Between the Internet and the World Wide Web?

- ➲ How Does My E-mail Know Where to Go?

- ➲ How Long Is a Tweet?

A⁺

Smart Apple Media
P.O. Box 3263
Mankato, MN, 56002

First published in 2010 by
MACMILLAN EDUCATION AUSTRALIA PTY LTD
15–19 Claremont St, South Yarra, Australia 3141

Visit our web site at www.macmillan.com.au or go directly to www.macmillanlibrary.com.au

Associated companies and representatives throughout the world.

Copyright © Nicolas Brasch

Library of Congress Cataloging-in-Publication Data

Brasch, Nicolas.
    The Internet / Nicolas Brasch.
        p. cm. — (The technology behind)
    Includes index.
    ISBN 978-1-59920-567-0 (library bound)
    1. Internet—Juvenile literature. I. Title.
    TK5105.875.I57B725 2011
004.67'8—dc22

                    2009054445

Publisher: Carmel Heron
Managing Editor: Vanessa Lanaway
Editor: Georgina Garner
Proofreader: Erin Richards
Designer: Stella Vassiliou
Page layout: Stella Vassiliou and Raul Diche
Photo researcher: Wendy Duncan (management: Debbie Gallagher)
Illustrations by: Alan Laver, pp. 7, 19; Richard Morden, pp. 15, 28, 30; Karen Young, p. 1 and Try This! logo.
Production Controller: Vanessa Johnson

Manufactured in China by Macmillan Production (Asia) Ltd.
Kwun Tong, Kowloon, Hong Kong
Supplier Code: CP March 2010

Acknowledgements
The author and the publisher are grateful to the following for permission to reproduce copyright material:

Front cover photographs:
Child at computer © Steve Hix/Somos Images/Corbis; Text message © Cameron Spencer/Getty Images; Screenshot, www.google.com.

Courtesy of The Computer History Museum, **6** (top); © Richard Baker/Corbis, **8**; © Hannes Hepp/Corbis, **29**; © Steve Hix/Somos Images/Corbis, **21**; © Helen King/Corbis, **5**; © Push Pictures/Corbis, **31** (top); © Ed Quinn/Corbis, **14**; © Stephen Oliver/Dorling Kindersley/Getty Images, **18** (top centre); © Cameron Spencer/Getty Images, **24** (right); http://www.flickr.com/photos/jackdorsey/182613360/, **24** (left); Illustration for Kids, **22**; © Bogdan Dumitru/iStockphoto, **28**; © mikadx/iStockphoto, **18** (bottom centre); © Chris Schmidt/iStockphoto, **4**; www.mugglenet.com, **23**; Museum Victoria, **11**; http://history.sandiego.edu/gen/comp/images/Internet13.jp, **6** (bottom); © Shutterstock/AVAVA, **17**; © Shutterstock/Zhong Chen, **18** (bottom left); © Shutterstock/vospalej, **31** (bottom); UN Photo/Paulo Filgueiras, **18** (right); Webjet.com.au, **18** (top left); Reproduced with permission of Yahoo! Inc. ©2009 Yahoo! Inc. YAHOO! and the YAHOO! logo are registered trademarks of Yahoo! Inc., **16**.

Sources for quotes:
http://www.elon.edu/predictions/prediction2.aspx?id=JQA-0058, **30** (left); http://www.elon.edu/e-web/predictions/expertsurveys/2008survey/internet_time_work_leisure_2020.xhtml, **31** (both); http://www.livinginternet.com/i/ia_future.htm, **30** (centre); http://pewresearch.org/pubs/1053/future-of-the-internet-iii-how-the-experts-see-it, **30** (bottom); http://www.scientificamerican.com/article.cfm?id=the-semantic-web, **27**.

Sources for web pages:
www.google.com 13 (all), **26**; http://www.nasa.gov, **12**; http://www.panda.org, **10** (top and bottom); http://twitter.com/BARACKOBAMA, **25** (top); http://twitter.com/lancearmstronG, **25** (bottom); http://en.wikipedia.org/wiki/Main_Page, **27**; http://simple.wikipedia.org/wiki/Tim_Berners-Lee, **9**.

While every care has been taken to trace and acknowledge copyright, the publisher tenders their apologies for any accidental infringement where copyright has proved untraceable. Where the attempt has been unsuccessful, the publisher welcomes information that would redress the situation.

The publisher would like to thank Heidi Ruhnau, Head of Science at Oxley College, for her assistance in reviewing manuscripts.

Please note
At the time of printing, the Internet addresses appearing in this book were correct. Owing to the dynamic nature of the Internet, however, we cannot guarantee that all these addresses will remain correct.

▶ Contents

Look out for these features throughout the book:

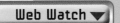

"Word Watch" explains the meanings of words shown in **bold**

Web Watch ▼

"Web Watch" provides web site suggestions for further research

What Is Technology?

The First Tools

One of the first examples of technology, where humans used their knowledge of the world to their advantage, was when humans began shaping and carving stone and metals into tools such as axes and chisels.

▲ People use technology every day, such as when they turn on computers. Technology is science put into action to help humans and solve problems.

Technology is the use of **science** for practical purposes, such as building bridges, inventing machines, and improving materials. Humans have been using technology since they built the first shelters and lit the first fires.

Technology in People's Lives

Technology is behind many things in people's everyday lives, from lightbulbs to can openers. It has shaped the sports shoes people wear and helped them run faster. Cars, trains, airplanes, and space shuttles are all products of technology. Engineers use technology to design and construct materials and structures such as bridges, roads, and buildings. Technology can be seen in amazing built structures all around humans.

Technology is responsible for how people communicate with each other. Information technology uses scientific knowledge to determine ways to spread information widely and quickly. Recently, this has involved the creation of the Internet, and e-mail and file-sharing technologies. In the future, technology may become even more a part of people's lives, with the development of robots and artificial intelligence for use in business, in the home, and in science.

The Technology Behind the Internet and the World Wide Web

The Internet is both simple and complicated. It is simply a **network** of computers able to share information, but the technology behind it is very complex. The Internet has affected our day-to-day lives in many complex ways, too. In lots of ways, it has made the world smaller!

Bringing the World Closer Together

Throughout the ages, technology has brought communities closer together. In the past, the invention of new ships and steam trains made it easier to travel great distances, and new technologies such as the printing press, radio, and television meant that information could be distributed and broadcast across the world.

The Internet and the World Wide Web (WWW) have brought the world closer together in many ways. Some Internet **applications** have made the transfer of information faster, and others have made communication more mobile. Business people on opposite sides of the world can hold meetings in real time over the Internet. Friends can send instant messages to each other—and to millions of people they don't know, too. People can easily surf or search the World Wide Web for information or goods. They also place messages on the WWW when they blog, e-mail, or tweet.

▼ Due to the fast technological changes occurring with the Internet and the World Wide Web, many jobs of the future have not even been created yet!

The People Behind the Technology

Many people with different jobs and professions are behind the technology of the Internet and the World Wide Web.

Behavioral Researcher Studying how humans behave, such as how they **navigate** and use features on the Internet

Computer Scientist Designing hardware and software

Electrical Engineer Studying how electrical signals work, including how they can be sent through the air or through cables

Word Watch

applications programs or software that are written to perform particular jobs

navigate move from one Web page to another

network group or system of things that are connected

Web Watch ▼

www.internetworldstats.com/stats

5

How Was the Internet Invented?

The Internet was launched on October 29, 1969, when computers at two different sites in California were linked to each other. The **network** was called ARPANET (Advanced Research Projects Agency Network) and this small network eventually became the Internet.

Imagining the Internet

In 1962, J. C. R. Licklider from the Massachusetts Institute of Technology wrote about his idea for a "galactic network" of computers that would allow people to access information from linked computers. Licklider worked with other computer scientists over the next few years, trying to make this idea a reality. They concentrated on developing a technology called "**data** switching," which allows data to be broken down into small packages and sent through a computer network to various destinations. By the late 1960s, various packet switching trials had been successful. The linking of computers in the ARPANET network soon followed.

Internet = Interconnected
The name "Internet" was introduced as a shortened way of describing an interconnected system of networks.

Word Watch

data information that has been translated into electronic signals that can be moved from one place to another

network group or system of things that are connected

protocol set of rules that control the exchange of electronic data

▶ Computers at the University of California (UCLA) and at the Stanford Research Institute (SRI) were the first to be connected to ARPANET. A month later, computers at the University of Santa Barbara (UCSB) and the University of Utah (UTAH) joined the network.

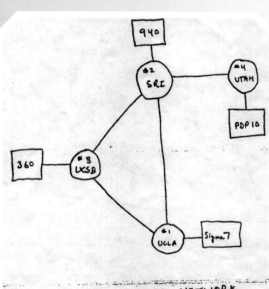

THE ARPA NETWORK

DEC 1969

4 NODES

Slow Progress

Only a couple of hundred computers were added to ARPANET between 1969 and 1979, but computer scientists around the world were figuring out how to link other networks to ARPANET. All the networks were different, and they needed a common **protocol** to link together. By 1982, a protocol had been developed and the Internet, as it was now called, began to boom.

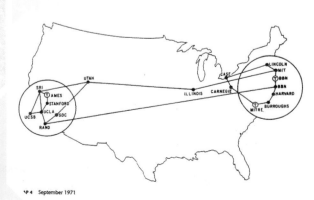

▶ More computers across the United States joined ARPANET by September 1971.

\P 4   September 1971

Web Watch ▼

www.elon.edu/e-web/
predictions/150/1960.xhtml

How the Internet Works

Every computer that is linked to the Internet is a part of the Internet. The Internet does not feed information back to one huge computer. It is made up of all the computers that link it together.

To link to the Internet, a person needs a computer, a **modem**, and usually a telephone line or cable. People using wireless modems do not need a telephone line or cable. Once these things are linked together, the computer can make contact with an Internet service provider (ISP). The ISP acts as the gateway to the Internet.

In businesses, schools, and governments, the computers in one location or within one organization are often linked first to a local area network (LAN). They gain their access to the Internet through the LAN, which is connected to the Internet.

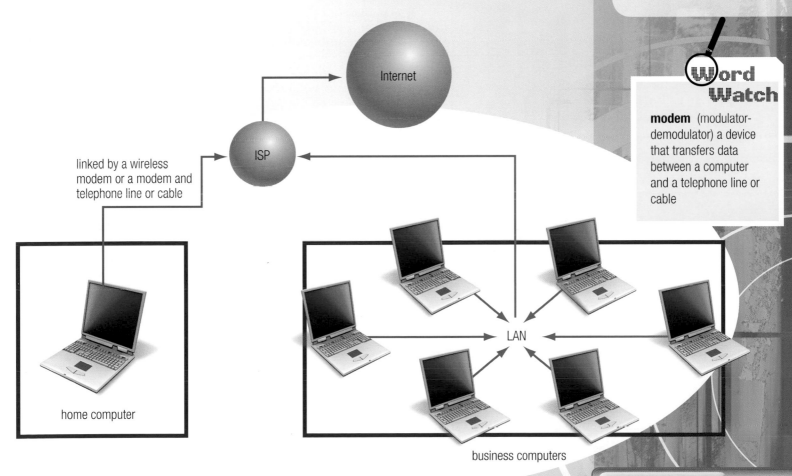

Internet

ISP

linked by a wireless modem or a modem and telephone line or cable

home computer

LAN

business computers

▲ Computers can use a modem with a telephone line or cable, or a wireless modem to link to the Internet.

What Is the Difference Between the Internet and the World Wide Web?

Many people think that the World Wide Web and the Internet are the same thing—but they aren't. The WWW is one way of viewing, hearing, and transferring information over the Internet.

Before the World Wide Web

The Internet started in 1969, but the WWW was not created until 1990. Before the creation of the WWW, there were no pictures, sound, movie clips, or links from one page to another on the Internet.

In 1990, Tim Berners-Lee, a British computer scientist, developed a way of accessing information on the Internet more easily, called Hypertext Markup Language (HTML). In 1991, he announced that other people could use and contribute to this World Wide Web project.

▲ Before 1990, there were many different ways to display and access information on the Internet, and users had to go through complicated and time-consuming processes unless they knew exactly what they were looking for and where it was.

How the World Wide Web Works

The key to the WWW is a concept known as hypertext. Hypertext is a way to get from one piece of information to another. This linking concept has been around for decades, although it was not always called hypertext. If you look in an encyclopedia, many entries point the reader to other, related information within the same encyclopedia. This is an example of the "hypertext" concept.

Hypertext Markup Language (HTML)

Berners-Lee developed a computer language called Hypertext Markup Language (HTML), which allowed information to be displayed on the Internet in many different formats. Clicking on an image could set off a function that turned the image into a moving image with sound. HTML also allowed users to click on links that took them to other Web pages or even other sites.

The collection of pages that display information using HTML is called the World Wide Web. HTML and the WWW revolutionized the way the Internet was used and who used it. More World Wide Web pages were added and more people began to use the Internet. WWW became the most popular way of accessing information.

Tim Berners-Lee also came up with the idea for uniform resource locators (**URLs**), as a way of easily finding particular pages, such as www.nasa.gov and www.australiazoo.com.au.

Web of Communication
Tim Berners-Lee thought of different names for his creation before deciding on World Wide Web. He considered "Mesh" and "The Information Mine." He chose World Wide Web because he saw that people and organizations communicated in a web-like fashion, not necessarily through a central point.

▼ HTML allows both words and images to work as hyperlinks.

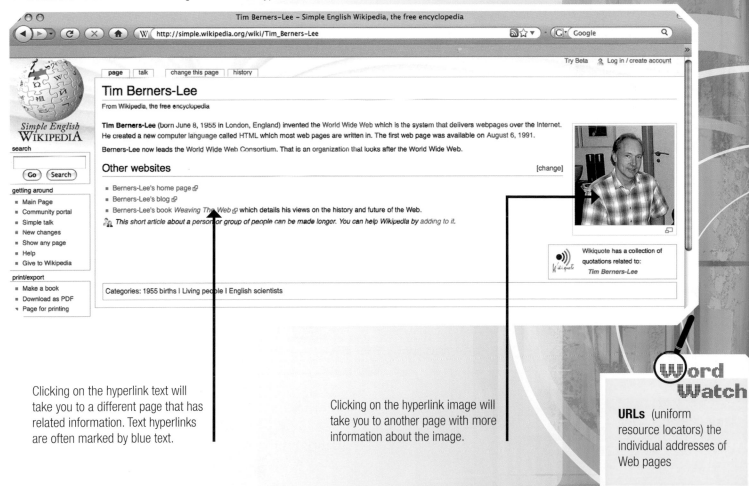

Clicking on the hyperlink text will take you to a different page that has related information. Text hyperlinks are often marked by blue text.

Clicking on the hyperlink image will take you to another page with more information about the image.

Word Watch
URLs (uniform resource locators) the individual addresses of Web pages

What Are Web Browsers?

The First Web Browsers

The first commercial Web browser was Mosaic. It was created by Marc Andreessen and Eric Bina, two American computer science students, and it was released in 1993. They improved the browser and then relaunched it under the name Netscape Navigator. Netscape Navigator was the most popular Web browser for several years until Microsoft launched Internet Explorer.

A Web browser is a program that makes web site **data** understandable for World Wide Web users. It translates computer language into the text and images seen on a Web page. The most commonly used Web browser is Internet Explorer.

Converting HTML into a Web Page

Web pages and web sites are written in a computing language known as Hypertext Markup Language (HTML; see page 8). HTML includes the information that is to appear on a web site, but this information is contained within lines and lines of coded instructions. A Web browser converts this code and translates it so that only the information appears.

Try This!

Look At a Web Page's HTML

To see what a Web page looks like in HTML, rather than converted by a Web browser, open a Web page and follow these instructions.

Steps

1. Type in a **URL** for a web site or **navigate** to a Web page.

2. Go to the View menu and choose "View source" or "Page source" (the wording of the instruction will depend on the Web browser you are using).

3. The text that appears is for the same Web page but it is written in HTML.

4. Click the window closed and you will return to your Web page.

Rare tiger cubs sniff WWF camera

1

3

Different Web Browsers for Different Computers

There are several different Web browsers that people use to **surf** the Internet. The most popular is Internet Explorer but others are Firefox, Opera, and Safari. Some of these Web browsers can be used only on personal computers (PCs), some on just Mac computers, and some on all types of computer.

Features of Web Browsers

Web browsers use some or all of the following features.

Toolbar

The toolbar features buttons to navigate around the WWW, such as "back" and "refresh" buttons.

Address Bar

This appears below the title bar and features the address of the Web page, called the URL.

Title Bar

This appears at the very top of the browser window and features the title of the Web page.

Status Bar

This box at the bottom of the Web browser window displays information such as the speed of the Internet connection and the URL of a link that the **cursor** is hovering over.

Display Window

This main area features the Web page and its information.

Scroll Bar

This allows users to move the Web page up and down to see more information.

Word Watch

cursor indicator on a computer screen

surf move from site to site on the Internet

How Does a Search Engine Work?

▶ A bot, Web crawler, or spider gathers only certain information about a Web page. It relies on the fact that the most important information is near the top of the page, such as the words shown circled in red.

There are millions of web sites and billions of Web pages on the World Wide Web. Finding particular information would be almost impossible without a tool that searches through these pages. This tool is called a search engine. The most used search engine is Google.

Creating Search Engines

When the World Wide Web first began, companies, organizations, and individuals would send information about their new web sites to each company that was developing search engines. This information was then transferred into a massive **database**. People using a particular search engine would type in words related to the Web pages they were looking for. The search engine would list the options found in the database.

Bots, Web Crawlers, and Spiders

As the World Wide Web grew bigger, this method became too time consuming. Also, web site details that had not been submitted to the search engine were not being included in searches.

Search engine companies developed **devices** known as bots, Web crawlers, and spiders that "crawl" the World Wide Web and collect information. This information includes keywords, the number of times these keywords appear, the position and size of these words, the number of links on a web site, and many other details about a Web page. These details are then put into the search engine's database so that they are included in searches.

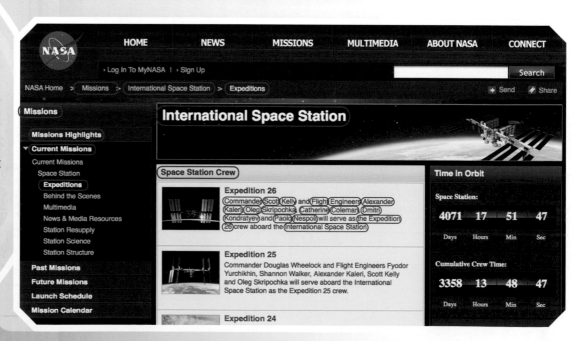

Search Engine Rankings

It is important to companies and organizations that their pages appear close to the top of search engine rankings. They try to determine which keywords are likely to bring people to their site. They use these keywords as often as possible and close to the top of each page, so that search engines gather these details. They also add links to and from other web sites, because search engines use Web links as one of the **criteria** for Web page rankings.

Try This!

Comparing Different Searches

A search depends on words and instructions that you give the search engine. Follow these steps to try out different searches.

Steps

1. Narrow your search as much as possible. For example, if you are doing an assignment on the Amazon river, entering the words "Amazon" and "river" will produce better results than entering "South America" and "river" or just "Amazon."

1

2. Most search engines use Boolean logic to make a search more specific. For example, users can put the words "AND" or "OR" between keywords to narrow or widen a search. Entering "Amazon AND river" gives Web pages that contain both keywords, making it more likely that your search will bring up relevant Web pages. Entering "Amazon OR trees" will bring up Web pages that contain either of these words. This will result in many more Web pages being found, although some of them may not be relevant.

2

3. You can also narrow your search by typing in a key phrase. You do this by using double quotation marks. For example, entering "Amazon river" will bring up just those Web pages that use this complete phrase. This makes it very likely that the pages will be relevant.

3

Web Watch ▼

www.internettutorials.net/boolean.asp

How Does My E-mail Know Where to Go?

E-mail is short for "electronic mail." E-mail **applications** enable messages to be sent from person to person over the Internet. Different e-mail programs work together because of a universally recognized address system and **protocols** for sending, receiving, and storing messages.

The Invention of E-mail

Before e-mail was invented, people could communicate with each other over the Internet but they had to be connected to the same computer. Shortly after the launch of the Internet (then known as ARPANET; see page 6), American computer scientist Ray Tomlinson set about creating a way to send messages to anyone connected to the Internet.

In 1971, Tomlinson sent the first e-mail message over the Internet between two computers that were not connected to each other. The message did not travel far. He sent it to himself from one computer to another in the same building. Within just 12 months, e-mail became the most popular application on the Internet.

(see page 6)

The First E-mail Message

The e-mail message that Ray Tomlinson sent to himself was so unimportant that he cannot remember what it said. There are reports that it said "Testing 1-2-3" but others that it said "QWERTYUIOP."

▲ Ray Tomlinson created the protocols that are still used by e-mail systems today, such as using "@" in addresses.

Word Watch

applications programs or software that are written to perform particular jobs

protocols sets of rules that control the exchange of electronic data

Protocols and Addresses

The key to Tomlinson's invention was that it had protocols to send, receive, and store the messages, and a common addressing system. The protocols he developed are known as Simple Mail Transfer Protocol (SMTP) and Post Office Protocol (POP). SMTP is responsible for sending the e-mail to the desired address, while POP is responsible for the retrieval and storage of the e-mail.

▼ Tomlinson's addressing system breaks an e-mail address into two parts. The two parts are separated by the symbol @.

nicolas47@myschool.edu

The local part of the address is usually the name or another identification of the account holder

The second part of the address is the domain name of the company, organization, or host server

The @ Symbol
The symbol @ that is used in e-mails is read as "at." There is no name for this symbol other than to call it "at."

Word Watch

server huge computer that allows other computers to access data, e-mail, and other network services

From One Destination to Another

This is how an e-mail is sent from one destination to another.

1. The sender types a message in her e-mail program, as well as the address of the person she is sending the e-mail to, called the recipient. She presses the "send" button. The message then goes to the mail user agent (MUA) of the sender.

4. The recipient opens the e-mail program on his computer, or presses the receive button on the e-mail program, and the e-mail is delivered. The recipient reads the e-mail.

To: marco@doogle.com
From: alicia@achoo.com
Hi Marco! ...

To: marco@doogle.com
From: alicia@achoo.com
Hi Marco! ...

SMTP

POP3

The Internet

smtp.achoo.com

mx.doogle.com
pop3.doogle.com

SMTP

Alicia's MUA

Marco's MUA

2. At the sender's MUA, the domain name in the recipient's address is noted and the MUA responsible for this domain name is identified. The e-mail is then sent to this MUA.

3. The recipient's MUA looks at the local part of the address and places the e-mail on its **server** ready to be "collected" by the recipient.

Web Watch ▼

www.learnthenet.com/english/
kids/120kids.htm

What Is Instant Messaging?

Instant messaging (IM) involves communicating **online** in real time with other people. Typed conversations between people are updated instantly. To communicate this way, users need special instant messaging software.

E-mail Versus Instant Messaging

E-mail became a popular form of communication because messages could be passed backward and forward in minutes, even seconds. It was cheaper than calling on the telephone and much quicker than sending a letter.

Eventually, however, users wanted to communicate even faster, in "real time." The introduction of instant messaging meant that people no longer had to wait seconds or minutes for a response.

IM Technology

To use IM, users need to download to their computers an **application** known as a client. The client has its own identification and is connected to a general **server**.

Users indicate which people in their e-mail contact lists they want listed as "friends." The identification and contact details of these friends are recorded by the client, and users can see when their friends are online or **offline**. The users can now communicate directly with their friends through the server.

I Seek You
One of the most popular IM programs is ICQ, which is read as "I seek you."

Word Watch

application program or software that is written to perform a particular job

offline not connected to the Internet or the World Wide Web

online connected to the Internet or the World Wide Web

server huge computer that allows other computers to access data, e-mail, and other network services

▲ People can use an instant messaging service after downloading its client software.

Instant Messaging Features

Instant messaging services have many features. With IM people can:

- ➲ see if their friends are online or offline
- ➲ send and receive instant messages
- ➲ read old messages that they have sent or received
- ➲ enter a **chat room** to swap messages with others
- ➲ create a chat room for their friends to use
- ➲ send and view video clips
- ➲ send and receive files
- ➲ talk over the Internet, instead of over the telephone
- ➲ connect their IM program to their cell phone

IM and Business

Instant messaging is not just for personal communication and fun. Many businesses use IM to hold meetings between people in different locations. They also use IM to send files from one person to another.

▼ People can chat to family members who are far from home, using instant messaging.

Chat Room Rules

If you are invited into an IM chat room, make sure you know the person who is inviting you. Never let someone into your chat room unless you or a friend know who the new person is.

There are other rules you should observe in chat rooms:

- ➲ Do not use your real name as a nickname.
- ➲ Do not use a rude name as your nickname.
- ➲ Do not give out important personal details, such as your address.
- ➲ Do not ask others for important personal details.
- ➲ Do not type in capital or bold letters to attract attention. This is like yelling in the real world.

- ➲ If you get annoyed or angry, leave the chat room and cool down.
- ➲ Welcome new people to the chat room.
- ➲ Never agree to meet someone whom you have met in a chat room but who you do not know in real life.

Word Watch

chat room area on the Internet where users can communicate

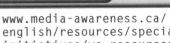

Web Watch ▼

www.media-awareness.ca/
english/resources/special_
initiatives/wa_resources/wa_
teachers/are_you_web_aware/
web_aware_im.cfm

www.bbc.co.uk/webwise/
askbruce/articles/chat/
instantmessage_1.shtml

What Do .Com, .Net, .Org, .Gov, .Mil, and .Edu Mean?

Typing in a **URL** is similar to addressing an envelope to go through the post. The URL is the address of the web site. The different parts of the URL mean different things.

Parts of a URL

At the end of a URL, there are usually two abbreviations separated by periods, such as ".gov.au." The first of these abbreviations is three letters long and explains what type of web site it is. This is known as a generic top-level domain (gTLD). The second abbreviation contains two letters and represents the country the site is based in. This is known as a country code top-level domain (ccTLD).

The First gTLDs

The first gTLDs were introduced in 1984. They were:

- ⮑ **.com** – short for commercial. This is the most common gTLD. It was originally intended for use by companies but it can now be used by anyone.

- ⮑ **.edu** – short for education. This gTLD is used by educational institutions such as schools, colleges and universities.

- ⮑ **.gov** – short for government. This is used by governments and government departments.

- ⮑ **.mil** – short for military. This is used only by the US Department of Defense.

- ⮑ **.org** – short for organization. This gTLD was intended for any group that did not fall into the other four categories.

www.webjet.com.au

▲ Webjet is a commercial company, so its website uses the .com gTLD.

www.harvard.edu

▲ Harvard University is an educational institution, so its URL includes .edu.

www.number10.gov.uk

▲ 10 Downing Street, London is the office of the English Prime Minister. This is an example of a government website.

www.pentagon.mil

▲ The U.S. Department of Defense have their own gTLD.

www.un.org

▲ The United Nations is an organization, so their URL includes the abbreviation .org.

Other gTLDs

Since 1998, other gTLDs have been approved for use. Most can only be used by the type of business or organization that they represent:

- ➲ .aero, for companies and organizations in the **aviation industry**
- ➲ .biz, for businesses or companies
- ➲ .coop, for cooperatives, which are organizations run by a group of individuals
- ➲ .info, for web sites providing information to the public
- ➲ .museum, for museums
- ➲ .name, for individuals
- ➲ .pro, for professionals such as lawyers and doctors

ccTLDs

Each country has its own ccTLD. The ccTLD of the United States is .us, but it is not often used. Instead, web sites based in the United States usually use a gTLD only, such as www.usa.gov.

Valuable ccTLD

In 2000, the Pacific Island nation of Tuvalu did a deal with a private company that gave the company use of Tuvalu's ccTLD. The company made the agreement because it thought that media companies would pay them a lot of money to put .tv at the end of their web site addresses.

Word Watch

aviation to do with flying and operating aircraft

industry activities concerned with making goods to sell, often in factories

▼ Each country has its own ccTLD, such as the examples shown here.

.se = Sweden
.gb and .uk = United Kingdom
.ru = Russian Federation
.it = Italy
.tr = Turkey
.ie = Ireland
.de = Germany
.ca = Canada
.es = Spain
.cn = China
.jp = Japan
.us = United States
.kr = Republic of Korea
.dz = Algeria
.in = India
.mx = Mexico
.ve = Venezuela
.vn = Vietnam
.pg = Papua New Guinea
.ne = Niger
.sa = Saudi Arabia
.pe = Peru
.br = Brazil
.cd = The Democratic Republic of the Congo
.sd = Sudan
.id = Indonesia
.au = Australia
.ar = Argentina
.ao = Angola
.nz = New Zealand
.za = South Africa
-N-
.aq = Antarctica

Spam filters stop unwanted e-mails arriving in people's e-mail inboxes. Internet filters stop users being able to access certain web sites from particular computers.

What Is Spam?

Spam is the name given to **unsolicited** e-mails. Some people jokingly say that SPAM stands for "Stupid Pointless Annoying Messages."

Spam e-mails are often sent to millions of e-mail addresses at the same time. Some spam e-mails ask for a person's bank account details. Their aim is to trick people out of money. The **spammers** do not expect many people to send them their account details but if just a few respond to the millions of e-mails they send out, they make money.

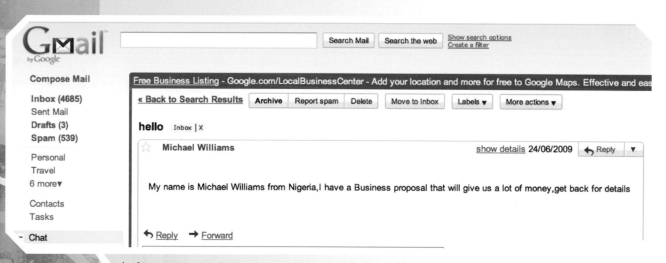

▲ Some spam e-mails promise people a great business deal if they send money now.

Filtering Spam

Without spam filters, people would be bombarded with messages! Many companies and individuals use these filters to sort genuine e-mails from spam e-mails. Filters do this by checking particular characteristics of e-mails, such as:

- ⮑ the words in the subject line
- ⮑ who sent the e-mail
- ⮑ images within the e-mail
- ⮑ the words in the e-mail body
- ⮑ the number of people within an organization who have been sent the same e-mail.

Some spam filters block and delete spam e-mails at the **server** of the Internet service provider (ISP). Other filters deliver spam e-mails to special junk folders where users can check them for themselves.

Word Watch

server huge computer that allows other computers to access data, e-mail, and other network services

spammers people or companies that send out spam e-mails

unsolicited sent without being requested

▼ Internet filters help parents protect children from inappropriate web sites.

What Is an Internet Filter?

An Internet filter is an **application** that stops users being able to access particular web sites. These web sites might be blocked because they feature inappropriate images or concepts, particularly for children.

How an Internet Filter Works

Internet filters work in one of four main ways.

Blacklists

A blacklist is a list of web sites that contain material not suitable for a particular audience. When someone tries to access a blacklisted web site, the filter recognizes the **URL** and will not display the site.

White Lists

A white list is similar to a blacklist, except that a white list contains the details of all the web sites that can be viewed. This is very limiting because the user cannot search for web sites not on the list, even if those sites are appropriate.

Keyword Blocks

An Internet filter with a keyword block has a list of words that it will not accept. Any web site that contains one or more of these words will not be displayed. The problem with a keyword block is that words can be used in different ways, and sites may be blocked even when they use a word in an appropriate way.

Ratings

A ratings filter uses a ratings system similar to those used for movies and television programs. A responsible person or a team of people view web sites and give them ratings. The filter is then set to accept only web sites with particular ratings. A web site that has not been rated will not be accepted.

Word Watch

application program or software that is written to perform a particular job

surfing moving from site to site on the Internet

URL (uniform resource locator) the individual address of a Web page

What Is the Difference Between a Blog and a Web Site?

There is very little difference in the way that a blog and a web site are set up and hosted. In fact, many web sites contain blogs. However, there is a lot of difference in the way they look, are updated, and are used.

What Is a Blog?

"Blog" is a shortened version of the word weblog. A blog is a web site or part of a web site that contains **commentary** and information that are regularly updated. The general content on a web site may only be updated every few months, but new content on a blog might be **posted** every few minutes or each day.

Different Types of Blogs

There are many different types of blogs. Some blogs are run by individuals who use them as **online** diaries that anyone can read. These blogs may contain comments on a range of topics, depending on what the **blogger** is doing or thinking on a particular day. Some blogs are dedicated to rock bands, football teams, books, or movies. These blogs contain comments on that topic only. Some blogs act as sources of information, urging people to ask questions that will then be answered by the owner of the blog or by other bloggers.

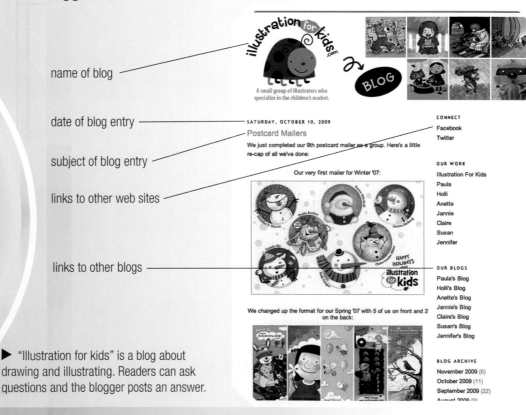

name of blog

date of blog entry

subject of blog entry

links to other web sites

links to other blogs

▶ "Illustration for kids" is a blog about drawing and illustrating. Readers can ask questions and the blogger posts an answer.

Plan Your Blog

Pretend you are setting up a blog. Follow the steps below to plan your blog's design and content.

Steps

1. Select a software program. There are many online software programs that help people set up blogs. Some are very simple and only offer a few basic features, while others are more complicated. Most people setting up a personal blog need only a simple option.

2. Select a name. The name should reflect the topic of the blog and should not be used by anybody else. Because there are so many blogs on the Internet, the most popular and obvious names have been taken.

3. The software programs have **templates** of different design options. Decide which design you like best.

4. Select the features. Consider whether or not you want features such as:

➲ contributions from other bloggers

➲ links to other blogs

➲ a "members only" section

➲ an e-mail link so people can contact you

5. Select a host. People who do not have great technological knowledge normally use a blog hosting service. Most companies that provide blogging software will also host the site on their **server**, in the same way that a web hosting service hosts web sites.

6. Start recording your thoughts and create a few sample blog entries. Share them with your family and friends.

More Types of Blogs

Blogs do not have to be just commentary and text.

➲ A blog that is mainly made up of video clips is called a vlog.

➲ A blog that is mainly made up of photos is called a photolog.

➲ A blog that mainly has links to other blogs is called a linklog.

Word Watch

server huge computer that allows other computers to access data, e-mail, and other network services

templates set formats for documents, files, or Web pages

▶ "Mugglenet" is a blog that has been created by fans of the Harry Potter books and films. You could create a fan blog, too.

Web Watch ▼

www.pbs.org/
mediashift/2006/05/
digging-deeperyour-guide-
to-blogging136.html

technorati.com/blogging/
state-of-the-blogosphere//

How Long Is a Tweet?

Twittering is like instant messaging, a web site, and a blog mixed together. Its most striking feature is that each message or "tweet" cannot be more than 140 characters long, including spaces. A person's tweets are all **posted** on the one web site.

Posting Tweets

Joining the world of Twitter is much easier than setting up a blog or a web site. New users simply set up their own profiles on the Twitter web site and then post their first messages. Users can also follow other twitters. This involves choosing "friends" and making a request to receive their messages as soon as they are posted. Whenever one of these friends posts a message, it is immediately posted on the Twitter pages of all those people who have signed up as his or her friend.

There are three main ways to post a message on Twitter. These are through the Twitter web site, using a cell phone, and through a Blackberry **device**.

Twitter Talk

Twitter has created some new words and phrases.

- ➲ People who post messages on Twitter are called "twitters."
- ➲ The messages that twitters post are called "tweets."
- ➲ RT stands for "retweet." This is when someone includes part of another person's tweet within his or her own tweet.

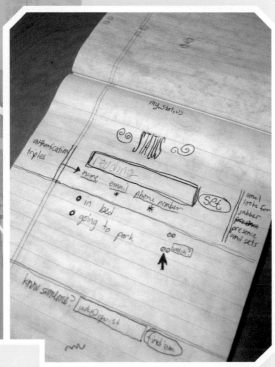

▲ Jack Dorsey spent more than five years developing his idea for Twitter. This notepaper shows some of his ideas.

▶ A person can post a tweet by sending a text message.

How Twitter Works

Twitter works using a process known as web syndication. This involves sending **data** from one **application** or source and distributing it to others. Web syndication makes it possible to **SMS** a tweet from a cell phone, have the tweet appear on the Twitter web site, and then have it transmitted in SMS form to the cell phones of all those registered to receive tweets from that particular twitter.

Tweets are limited to 140 characters because Twitter wanted to link SMS and Internet technologies, and SMS messages are limited to a certain number of characters—usually 160. The linking of technologies is also why tweets cannot contain images.

Who Uses Twitter?

Twitter started off as a way for people to keep their friends informed of the little things that were happening in their lives. Now, however, many celebrities and world leaders use Twitter, too. They use Twitter for two main reasons:

- ➲ to make sure that they stay in the public's attention
- ➲ to communicate their views and thoughts directly to their followers and fans

Some businesses use Twitter to inform customers as soon as a new product or service is available.

▲ President Barack Obama used Twitter to inform people and gather support during his campaign to become US president.

▶ Athletes and celebrities, such as cyclist Lance Armstrong, use Twitter to communicate with their fans.

Web Watch ▼

twitter.com

What Are Web 2.0 and Web 3.0?

Web 2.0 and Web 3.0 are used to describe new ways in which the Internet is used, both by businesses and individuals. The terms 2.0 and 3.0 represent the second and third generations of Internet technology, building on the original, basic **applications** of the Internet.

Early Internet

The early Internet is now sometimes referred to as Web 1.0. Before the early 2000s, the Internet was used mainly to display information. Businesses would list products and services, and government departments would give details of campaigns and projects. Few individuals created their own web sites. The ability to sell goods over the Internet was seen as a huge technological leap and many Internet companies, such as Amazon, became hugely successful.

Web 2.0

Some people wanted more out of the Internet and began to develop ideas and technology that **enhanced** the Internet experience for users. Rather than just searching for information and scanning Web pages, people could share information and **collaborate** with others over the Internet. This new approach became known as Web 2.0.

▲ The ability to upload images and videos to the Web is a key feature of Web 2.0.

Among the main features of Web 2.0 are:

- ⊃ search engines that accurately rank sites and information in order of importance
- ⊃ the ability for general users to change or add information on web sites
- ⊃ systems that alert users that new information is available to them
- ⊃ applications that make users feel they belong to a web site and are not just visitors

Examples of Web 2.0

Among the web sites that have sprung up over the past few years and which contain key Web 2.0 applications are:

- ⊃ Facebook
- ⊃ Flickr
- ⊃ MySpace
- ⊃ Twitter

- ⊃ Wikipedia (and other wiki sites)
- ⊃ YouTube
- ⊃ Youmeo

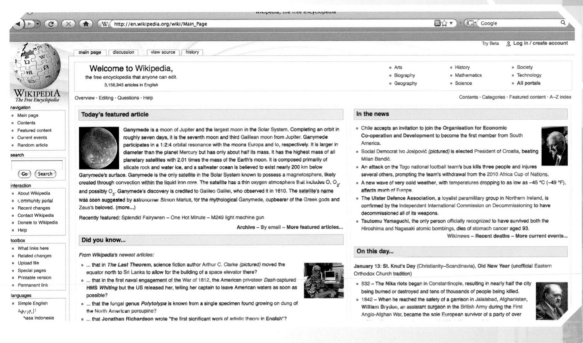

◄ Wikipedia is a free encyclopedia that is written and edited by Web users. This kind of application is typical of Web 2.0.

Web 3.0

Web 3.0 is sometimes called the Semantic Web. Tim Berners-Lee, the founder of the World Wide Web, is concentrating on creating Web 3.0 applications that enable computers to read information on the WWW and make choices for humans. In an article he cowrote, Berners-Lee explained how he sees Web 3.0 working. He writes that a woman called Lucy takes her mom to the doctor and is told that her mom has to see a specialist:

> "At the doctor's office, Lucy instructed her Semantic Web agent through her handheld Web browser. The agent promptly retrieved information about Mom's *prescribed treatment* from the doctor's agent, looked up several lists of *providers*, and checked for the ones ... within a *20-mile radius* of her *home* and with a rating of *excellent* or *very good* ..."

According to Berners-Lee, the meanings (semantics) of the words in italics will be defined first by Lucy, then Lucy's Semantic Web agent will be able to make decisions based on the information she gave it.

Web Watch ▼

www.scientificamerican.com/article.cfm?id=the-semantic-web

How Is Voice Over Internet Protocol Used?

Voice over Internet **Protocol** (VoIP) is the technology that enables people to speak over the Internet, much like people speak over the telephone. It works by **encoding** and **decoding** signals.

Encoding and Decoding Signals

VoIP works by converting sound into a **digital** form so that it can be sent along a cable or **broadband network**. The digital **data** is sent in small amounts known as packets. At the receiver's end, the digital data is decoded back into sound so that the receiver can hear what is being said.

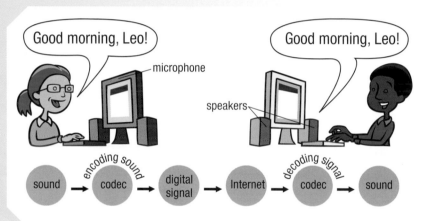

▲ VoIP technology uses coders and decoders called codecs to change sound into a digital signal and then back into sound.

Using VoIP

There are three main ways to use VoIP to communicate with other people: through an analog terminal adapter (ATA), using VoIP phones, or using computer-to-computer technology.

An analog terminal adapter connects an ordinary telephone to a computer or an Internet connection. Computer-to-computer is the cheapest method. It requires installing some software on a computer and having a microphone, speakers, and sound card in the computer. People on different computers can speak without paying phone charges, even if they are in different countries.

◀ VoIP phones are connected to the Internet through an ethernet connection that is plugged directly into a router or modem, or through a wireless connection.

Advantages and Disadvantages

There are advantages and disadvantages to using VoIP technology. Over time, some of the disadvantages will disappear as the technology improves.

The main advantages are:

- ➲ VoIP calls are cheaper to make than regular telephone calls
- ➲ VoIP is very mobile and calls can be made from anywhere in the world by logging on to the Internet
- ➲ computer users have their phone system available all the time

The main disadvantages are:

- ➲ VoIP networks are less reliable than regular telephone networks
- ➲ VoIP relies on many different parts and systems, and the failure of any one of these can end a call
- ➲ set-up costs may be more expensive than for regular telephone calls
- ➲ if the electricity goes out, VoIP stops working unless you are using battery power and wireless broadband. Regular telephone lines are not affected by electricity blackouts.

VVoIP

Another type of technology that is becoming more popular and more efficient is VVoIP. VVoIP stands for video and voice over Internet protocol. It involves the conversion of both images and sound into digital form so they can be transferred over the Internet.

Skype
The most popular VoIP **application** is Skype. More than 30 million people use Skype every day to make VoIP calls. The name Skype comes from the term "Sky peer-to-peer."

Word Watch

application program or software that is written to perform a particular job

◀ One major advantage of VVoIP technology is that businesses can hold meetings between people in different locations, rather than paying travel costs to get all the people in the same place.

Web Watch

www.iec.org/onlinc/
tutorials/int_tele/
topic01.asp

What Internet Technologies Will We Use in the Future?

Making predictions about any subject is always difficult. Making predictions about the Internet is particularly difficult, because things happen so quickly in the technological world of the Internet.

Looking to the Future

Companies, organizations, and government departments involved with the Internet regularly hold conferences to discuss the future of the Internet. Internet experts make predictions about new technologies and how people will use these technologies in their day-to-day lives.

Bringing the World Together

According to www.livingInternet.com, the distribution of information and knowledge through the Internet will become cheaper and cheaper. They predicted, "People will have access to any information they wish, get smarter sooner, and be more aware of the world outside their local environment." As a result, people's attachments to their own countries will decrease and "attachments to Earth as a shared resource will significantly increase."

Goodbye to Telephones

Other people predict the end of the telephone system. Josh Quittner, executive editor of *Fortune Magazine*, predicted that telephones would be old-fashioned and out-of-date by 2020. By that time, all **telephony** would be Internet-based and **devices** will use communication chips. He said, "We'll probably carry some kind of screen-based reading device that will perform this function, though I assume when we want to communicate verbally, we'll do so through a tiny, earplug-based device."

◄ Internet technologies are helping transform telephones.

Balancing Work, Life, and the Internet

Some experts, such as Rachel Kachur, a behavioral researcher, believe that work and home life are blending together due to the Internet and other technology. She said, "Technology allows us to **meld** both professional and personal and it will be increasingly hard to separate the two. Just like workers will pay bills **online** during 'work' hours, they will also attend to work over the dinner table. This will actually improve **productivity** and job satisfaction."

Some people do not see this as a positive thing. Computer scientist D. J. Strouse believes that within 10 years, people will want to escape the Internet and other technology. He said, "Communication-free zones [will be] established on resort, beachfront, and tropical properties and become popular tourist destinations. Digital communications [will not be] functional at these locations."

▲ Portable computers mean that people can bring their work home with them. This can be seen as a positive or a negative thing.

▶ Cell phones and laptop computers are banned in some areas, such as in some cafes, so that people can relax and not think about work.

Word Watch

meld mix
online connected to the Internet or the World Wide Web
productivity efficiency and quality with which a job gets done

Index